The Three A's of Today's Teens:

Restoring the Brokenness of Today's Generation

by Omar Lee Miranda

© 2018

The older Apostle Paul's first letter to his younger protégé, Timothy:

"Don't let anyone look down on you because you are young, but set an example for the believers in speech, in conduct, in love, in faith and in purity. Until I come, devote yourself to the public reading of Scripture, to preaching and to teaching. Do not neglect your gift, which was given you through prophecy when the body of elders laid their hands on you.

Be diligent in these matters; give yourself wholly to them, so that everyone may see your progress. Watch your life and doctrine closely. Persevere in them, because if you do, you will save both yourself and your hearers."

--1 Timothy 4: 12-16, NIV

"You have made us for yourself, and restless is our heart until it comes to rest in you."

--Augustine, *The Confessions*

" . . . Creatures are not born with desires unless satisfaction for those desires exists. A baby feels hunger: well, there is such a thing as food. A duckling wants to swim: well, there is such a thing as water. Men feel sexual desire: well, there is such a thing as sex. If I find in myself a desire which no experience in this world can satisfy, the most probable explanation is that I was made for another world."

"God cannot give us a happiness and peace apart from Himself, because it is not there. There is no such thing."

--C.S. Lewis, *Mere Christianity*

Dedication

I want to dedicate this book to three groups of people:

1. My parents: who never, EVER stopped praying for me—even in the midst of my foolish and stupid decisions. I love you, Mami & Papi

2. My wife and children: all three of you are my world! I could not have written this book without your love, patience, insights, and encouragement. I love you Renee, Isabella & Jackson.

3. For all the people—counselors, and otherwise—who have it made it their life's mission to minister to teenagers. May God richly bless you, your families, and your varied ministries.

Acknowledgements

Blame Carmela Monk Crawford, editor of the *phenomenal* magazine, *Message* (https://www.messagemagazine.com) for this book! The fault rests squarely on her shoulders!

Several months ago she and I were chatting and I was recounting incredible and miraculous story after story of how God's Holy Spirit power had worked in many of my client's lives; following a brief pause in the conversation, she asked me about my process. That got me to thinking and I realized that I didn't really have a process—at least not a formal one that was written, systematic, and clear.

Out of that conversation, you have before you: this book.

Thank you Carmela for being such a wonderful listener and asking such insightful and incisive questions.

May God continue to bless you, your family, and the life-changing ministry of *Message* magazine.

Table of Contents

Introduction

In over twenty years of community counseling experiences I have *NEVER* seen so many teenagers (Christian & non-Christian) in such bad shape! If something drastic, comprehensive, and consistent isn't done to meet their needs, they won't be able to live a life that is happy, healthy, and a blessing to others. Without emergency interventions a vast majority of teens will either be incarcerated, unemployed, addicted, or dead!

Approximately one out of five adolescents has a diagnosable mental health disorder.[1] And the numbers continue to rise. Which makes working with them very challenging, but I can think of no other group that is more rewarding. The greatest thing about working with this age group is the fact that *they are not children*, so they already know how they feel about something, and unlike younger children, can usually express it with words and feelings. Also, they *are not adults*, so their coping skills and habits haven't yet been set in stone and, therapeutically speaking, it's easier to affect positive and lasting change.

In my experience, the one thing that is consistent in most of the teens I have worked with is that they have been psychologically/emotionally traumatized in some way, shape, or form. What is a trauma, you may ask? Well, simply put, it is defined as ". . . [when] a person's spirit, and sometimes the will to live, as well as beliefs about the world and oneself, dignity, sense of security, thinking, and feeling have all been impacted."[2] When this happens their usual stress coping skills are inadequate.

Unfortunately, this means that they are all damaged goods! In over 20 years, I have seen teens go from having "normal" teen issues to consistently having serious problems with:

1. Depression

2. Anxiety

3. Reactive Attachment Disorder

4. Impulse Control Problems like: Oppositional Defiant Disorder; Conduct Disorder; Intermittent Explosive Disorder & Disruptive Mood Dysregulation Disorder, to name some of the most extreme.

These issues manifest themselves in behaviors like:

1. Anger management problems

2. Addictions

3. Gang Involvement

4. Early Sexual Initiation/Pregnancy/STDs

5. Educational Problems

6. Criminal Activities

7. Laziness/Serial Unemployment

8. Lack of Becoming an Adult

9. Suicidal Thoughts/Actions

10. Relationship Problems

Before we go any further I need to clarify that this book is written primarily for Christians who love, know, work with, and have a concern for reaching out to *non-Christian* teens. In this book I discuss information, ideas, and resources from my experiences and training as a Counselor, but you don't have to be one to read, understand, and effectively use this information. However, I know that these principles and practices will also be effective for those who are Christians as well.

If you are a parent, family member, friend, or just someone who has a heart for helping teenagers, I would highly recommend that you seriously consider what I consider the best and most comprehensive Christian counseling course available (no, they haven't paid me money for me to write this about them) to someone who doesn't want to become a professional counselor: "Caring for Teens God's Way" by the American Association of Christian Counseling's (AACC) educational organization, Light University. I have a Certificate in Biblical Counseling from this organization and for many years, was a member, and there is no finer or more qualified educational institution. You can learn more about it here: https://bit.ly/2I77Gux or by calling them at 1 (877) 506-LU4U (*5848)* or emailing them at: Admissions@LightUniversity.com

I'm Sorry in Advance (Not Really)

Before we really get into the book, I must apologize.

Let me explain.

The mission that we are about to embark on is a serious and crucial one! And a mission as serious as this requires *serious* training and preparation. Therefore, I'm going to hit you with a lot of information, theories, and resources. Even though I worked real hard to keep the tone of the book as light and conversational as possible, it's likely that you may feel like you are in school. I'm sorry…but not really. I'm not being mean—really. All I can say is "hang in there!"

God made people—yes, even *teenage* people—in His image! In fact, in all of God's creation, people and relationships are the most important thing to Him; if you are a Christian (which I hope you are)—then helping/improving people and their relationships should be important to you as well. Here's the bottom-line: I would not have included this information if I didn't absolutely feel that it was necessary.

Before I dive into what I think the solution needs to be, I think it's wise for you to know a little bit more about who I am and why I feel so strongly about this issue.

Chapter 1: A Little About Me

I believe that God has uniquely gifted and prepared me to fulfill the role of Pastor for Youth/YA ministries. I have my Master's in Community Counseling, an Initial Certification in School Counseling and am a recovering sex & porn addict. I have over 25 years of direct youth and ministry experience working with youth and their families in all aspects and venues.

I am a strong Seventh-day Adventist (SDA) Christian. I was raised in a strong SDA Christian household. I hail from a third-generation SDA family; a proud line of strong faith, beliefs, and quirky-lifestyle practices. I witnessed both of my parents having strong personal relationships with Jesus. We had worship and devotions twice a day. My parents did everything right. I was even raised in an area of the U.S. where there was a large conglomeration of SDA's—some have called this an SDA ghetto. Here, I was exposed to a lot of church. I went through Bible studies and was baptized at the tender young age of 8.

In my community, there were a lot of SDA churches, an SDA elementary school and academy. Anytime the church doors were opened, I was there. I went through everything the SDA church had to offer: Pathfinders (similar to Boys & Girls Scouts), academy (SDA high school), summer camp, and all that went with it. I was the poster-boy for a good SDA, but I never got it for myself. I saw it with others. Many people had so-called relationships with Jesus, but only a few had real relationships with Him and even fewer actually talked with me transparently about the joys and struggles of the Christian life.

I started walking away from Christ around the 7th grade. I was around 13 or 14 years old. I can't tell you that any one thing did it for me. Looking back on it and thinking about it for a long time, I've realized that it was a combination of several important things:

1. I never had consistent contact, saw or had an ongoing relationship with a lot of people that had a vibrant, joyful, authentic Christian experience. People who were honest about their struggles, ups, and downs. E.G. White writes this convicting statement: "It is because so many parents and teachers profess to believe the Word of God while their lives deny its power, that the teaching of Scripture has no greater effect upon the youth." (*Education*, p. 259)

2. I was never really taught how to have a vibrant relationship with Jesus. What I mean by that was that I was never taught practical Christianity aka How to live life in the Spirit vs. the flesh, how does one make faith practical in real life. I remember hearing stories about Jesus being in "constant communion with God" and I even remember reading about Jesus in Desire of Ages about when He was on the cross, the thing that

almost killed Him was having His relationship cut off and being apart from God. I remember thinking "so what?! What's the big deal?!" I didn't get it, because I didn't have it. I didn't figure out that I could successfully access the power of the Holy Spirit to overcome bad habits and sin in my life until I was in the midst of overcoming an addiction to sex and pornography.

I wish I would have been taught as a child, teen and college student, but alas, I had to learn it all the hard way! I was raised in a strong, bible-believing, God-worshipping home where my parents respected, honored and obeyed God, but I didn't see the same example in a lot of people from my church; what I saw was predominantly a bible-believing, doctrine-teaching, HARD church and a lot of hypocritical, miserable, mean people. There was a lot of truth, but not a lot of love. There was lots of judgment and condemnation and little to no understanding, grace, forgiveness, discernment, kindness or authenticity. I saw a lot of people that were afraid…afraid of being honest, afraid of being real, afraid of calling themselves sinners and imperfect. I was taught all the right and wrongs, but I wasn't taught the "hows." I was never taught practical Christianity. You know; how to live life as a Christian--and succeed!

Due to all the foolish life choices I made beginning in middle school—and onward, I have always had a special place in my heart for working with teenagers—because I know that during these important and difficult transitional years, many of them "go off the rails" in their lives.

Due to my…life "experiences" I am a recovering food/sex/pornography addict. Because of all of that I decided to ultimately get my Master's degree in Community Mental Health Counseling, and have been working with kids/teens, their families, and their communities for all these years.

I seek to fulfill God's calling upon my life, given to me on November of 1999, to enter full-time youth/young adult ministry. In the early 2000s my wife and I both completed an intensive and extensive two-year "Lay Pastor" training program. As I mentioned prior, I also completed a Certificate program in Christian Counseling as well as a Certificate in the Diagnosis & Treatment of Sex/Pornography Addictions. I have also written eight books and one short story, and when the Holy Spirit allows me to share that information in the course of my counseling time (of course only after the client(s) clearly prompt the conversation), I do.

Therefore, I believe with all my heart that the position of community counselor that God has placed me in has allowed me the opportunity and honor of full-time youth ministry; a ministry that, frankly, is crucial, because a vast majority of these teens and their families will likely never step foot into a church.

By the way, if you have any comments or questions (or answers—I could always more of those) feel free to write me at: omarmiranda@comcast.net or you can learn more about me on my web-site: http://omarmiranda4.wixsite.com/mirandawrites

The Why & How I Share Jesus With Them

<u>My Life Purpose</u>

1. To use everything I have and am to help youth/young adults to better: "Know Jesus » Love Jesus » Live Jesus." (John 12:32; Luke 10:27 & Philippians 3:7-12

2. To use everything I have and am to help youth/young adults to become mature Christians (Col. 1:25-28)

3. To use everything I have and am to help youth/young adults to be examples to others by ministering to others and leading in their local church and in their lives. (1 Timothy 4:11-16)

<u>My Mission & Vision</u>

Mission: "Know Jesus » Love Jesus » Live Jesus."

Vision: To educate, equip, inspire, advocate for & encourage youth and those that love them by:

1. telling our youth about Jesus, introducing them to Him, teaching them how to love Him more and know Him better, encouraging and training them how to think and live like Christians, and to effectively share Him with others and
2. moving those that love youth to honestly and consistently connect with them

I've told you all that to tell you why I feel so strongly focused in my work helping teens and young adults:

1.   Fall in love with Jesus Christ and give Him their hearts, their wills, their alls and then follow Him all the days of their lives!

2.   Grow and flourish in their relationship with God, through Jesus.

3.   Not make stupid mistakes that get them tangled up in years and years of chronic sin, addictions, bad life choices and the consequences that go with them. Instead they'll be able to sidestep those things and

4.   Share that love and freedom that they've found in Christ with as many people as they can to

5.   Speed Christ's return so we can all go home to spend eternity with Jesus, God & The Holy Spirit.

My Evangelism Method

> Christ's method alone will give true success in reaching the people. The Saviour mingled with men as one who desired their good. He showed His sympathy for them, ministered to their needs, and won their confidence. Then He bade them, 'Follow Me.' There is need of coming close to the people by personal effort. If less time were given to sermonizing, and more time were spent in personal ministry, greater results would be seen. The poor are to be relieved, the sick cared for, the sorrowing and the bereaved comforted, the ignorant instructed, the inexperienced counseled. We are to weep with those that weep, and rejoice with those that rejoice. Accompanied by the power of persuasion, the power of prayer, the power of the love of God, this work will not, cannot, be without fruit" (E. G. White, *The Ministry of Healing*, pp.143, 144).

Re-Programming Teens' Minds

In being able to share Jesus with all my clients, my goal is to allow God, His Word, the Bible, and His Holy Spirit to "re-program" them so to speak and replace all the "truths" they've believed about themselves, others, and the world, through the trauma they've witnessed/experienced in their lives and the lies they see presented by popular culture. In order to do that, I have found no better model for than the one below. It is built on four simple strands:

> **I. Practical Theology/Spiritual Formation**: How to Know Christ & How to Live in Power, Peace & Purpose as a Christian day by day
> **II. Doctrine**: What to Believe
> **III. Worldview/Apologetics**: Why to Believe, Why You Believe & How to Think & Process Information Christianly/Biblically
> **IV. Evangelism**: How to Effectively Share What You Believe & Make Disciples for Jesus

In addition, I also subscribe to Pastor Andy Stanley's principles as listed in his book *The Seven Checkpoints for Student Leaders* (2011). In his book, he states that there are seven irreducible principles that teens should be taught which will allow them to not only live happy, long, productive lives, but will also maximize their usefulness and effectiveness for God for this world and the next. They are:

#1 **Authentic Faith**: Putting Your Trust in God
#2 **Spiritual Disciplines**: Seeing With God's Eyes
#3 **Moral Boundaries**: Paving The Way for Intimacy
#4 **Healthy Friendships**: Choosing Friends for Life. Determining the Quality & Direction of our Lives.
#5 **Wise Choices**: Walking Wisely in a Fool's World
#6 **Ultimate Authority**: Finding Freedom Under God. Maximum Freedom Comes when we Submit to the Ultimate Authority.
#7 **Others First**: Considering Others Before Yourself

Chapter 2: Understanding Teens

My Philosophical, Theoretical & Theological Perspectives on Teenagers' Views on God & Spirituality

God is a being who is in community and He designed us all with the core need for connection and community with Him.

I find it interesting that Jesus softly calls to us and knocks on the doors of our hearts (Rev. 3:20) in order to extend an invitation to have connection with Him, but many times His call to us is drowned out by all we think the world has to offer: money, sex, power, position & prestige (1 John 2:15:16).

Jesus makes it clear that we cannot both love God and love the world. But I am convinced that the devil has fooled us--especially our youth into thinking that God is somebody who is to be afraid of, not somebody to be a friend of. The devil did the same thing to Adam and Eve in the Garden of Eden. Right after they sinned, God came looking for them. Genesis 3: 8-10 states:

> Then the man and his wife heard the sound of the Lord God as he was walking in the garden in the cool of the day, and they hid from the Lord God among the trees of the garden. But the Lord God called to the man, "Where are you?" He answered, "I heard you in the garden, and I was afraid because I was naked; so I hid" (NIV).

We've been hiding from God ever since. The devil has fooled people into thinking that God's someone who is here to take their fun and freedom away from them, but the only way they can truly have fun, freedom, fulfillment, power, purpose and peace is doing life God's way. The Apostle Paul asks this logical question to the Romans:

> When you were slaves of sin, you didn't have to please God. But what good did you receive from the things you did? All you have to show for them is your shame, and they lead to death. Now you have been set free from sin, and you are God's slaves. This will make you holy and will lead you to eternal life. Sin pays off with death. But God's gift is eternal life given by Jesus Christ our Lord (Romans 6:20-23, CEV).

Solomon, the wisest man EVER, spent almost his entire life searching for fulfillment and meaning. In his frustration—but to our benefit—he wrote everything he learned down in his diary, and we have it in the form of the Biblical Old Testament book called Ecclesiastes. Solomon starts his diary on a promising note stating that everything in life is a waste of time:

> Nothing makes sense! Everything is nonsense. I have seen it all—nothing makes sense! What is there to show for all of our hard work here on this earth? People come, and people go, but still the world never changes. The sun comes up, the sun goes down; it hurries right back to where it started from. The wind blows south, the wind blows north; round and round it blows over and over again. All rivers empty into the sea, but it never spills over; one by one the rivers return to their source. All of life is far more boring than words could ever say. Our eyes and our ears are never satisfied with what we see and hear. Everything that happens has happened before; nothing is new, nothing under the sun. Someone might say, "Here is something new!" But it happened before, long before we were born. No one who lived in the past is remembered anymore, and everyone yet to be born will be forgotten too (Ecclesiastes 1:2-11, CEV).

Solomon spends 11 whole chapters talking about how foolish the search for fulfillment in this world is, but in the end of chapters 11 and in chapter 12 he gives us his conclusions--the answers he (and all of us) have been searching for. He gives us the secret of happiness, fulfillment, peace and satisfaction in life:

> I [Solomon] was a wise teacher with much understanding, and I collected a number of proverbs that I had carefully studied. Then I tried to explain these things in the best and most accurate way. Everything you were taught can be put into a few words: Respect and obey God! This is what life is all about. God will judge everything we do, even what is done in secret, whether good or bad (Ecclesiastes 12:9, 10, 13, 14, CEV).

It's important that we give youth the truth today as they seek to live their life with the knowledge that they can only find what they truly desire and need in God and God alone. Then they can say, like King David "My soul finds rest in God alone . . ." (Psalms 62:1, NIV) and "You, God, are my God, earnestly I seek you; I thirst for you, my whole being longs for you, in a dry and parched land where there is no water." (Psalms 63:1, NIV) "Satisfy us in the morning with your unfailing love, that we may sing for joy and be glad all our days" (Psalms 90:14, NIV). This term "unfailing love" is used 40 times in the NIV, and all instances refer to God! Because God's love will NEVER fail!

When God sees teens living their lives in search of things to satisfy their hunger for Him, He says "Don't..." but they run away angry from Him like little hurt and angry children throwing a temper tantrum, but if they were still long enough to listen to the rest of what He is trying to tell them, they would hear Him say, "Don't hurt yourself!" Sin always hurts us. The devil, ourselves, and this world, has fooled teens into thinking that it will help them. I truly believe if our youth truly understood the significance and power of *knowing Christ* and *being found in Him*, they would be standing in line to get into church the way people do to get the newest smart…thing!

Oh that our youth would turn to God for the peace, power, purpose & place that they are searching so hard for. They would eagerly say with David:

> I am determined to be faithful and to respect your laws. I follow your rules, Lord. Don't let me be ashamed. I am eager to learn all that you want me to do; help me to understand more and more. Point out your rules to me, and I won't disobey even one of them. Help me to understand your Law; I promise to obey it with all my heart. Direct me by your commands! I love to do what you say. Make me want to obey you, rather than to be rich. Take away my foolish desires, and let me find life by walking with you (Psalms 119:30-37, CEV).

When I actually began to be open to knowing Jesus--rather than just knowing about Him--I began to trust and love Him. When I began to love and trust Him, nothing was as important as seeking to know Jesus more and more deeply every day (Philippians 3:7-12). Things, relationships, other people...my sin! Nothing was as important as getting to know Jesus!

All of a sudden I began to think differently about my Christian walk. When tempted with sin, I went from a Sinner outlook: "Yeah! I'm gonna do that!" To someone who lives a Christian life outlook: "I shouldn't do that!" To, someone who has a love relationship with Jesus "I don't want to do that!" John Lilley insightfully stated: "'Legalistic remorse says, 'I broke God's rules,' while real repentance says, 'I broke God's heart.'"

I can always tell where a youth is in their relationship with Jesus by the questions they ask me. For instance, I've had many youth ask me, "Omar, I'm going out with my boyfriend/girlfriend. How far is too far? I mean, what is and isn't 'sinful sexual behavior?'" or another one that I often get asked "Omar, what about this movie, t.v. show, song, etc.? It's not too bad...there's just a little sex, bad language, violence, etc."

It's been my personal experience that when I skate as close to the edge of sin as I can, it's because I REALLY WANT TO SIN! The Apostle Paul Paul wrote this sad thing to the Christians at Philippi:

" I often warned you that many people are living as enemies of the cross of Christ. And now with tears in my eyes, I warn you again that they are headed for hell! They worship their stomachs and brag about the disgusting things they do. All they can think about are the things of this world" (Philippians 3:18, 19, CEV). The Apostle John wrote these piercing and convicting words to Christians as well:

> You know that Christ came to take away sins. He isn't sinful, and people who stay one in their hearts with him won't keep on sinning. If they do keep on sinning, they don't know Christ, and they have never seen him. Children, don't be fooled. Anyone who does right is good, just like Christ himself. Anyone who keeps on sinning belongs to the devil. He has sinned from the beginning, but the Son of God came to destroy all that he has done. God's children cannot keep on being sinful. His life-giving power lives in them and makes them his children, so that they cannot keep on sinning. You can tell God's children from the devil's children, because those who belong to the devil refuse to do right or to love each other (1 John 3:5-10, CEV).

As I've said before, it's one thing to be focused on knowing Christ more and more and in the midst of that relationship to stumble and sin, but John, in this passage, is speaking of people who knowingly and blatantly continue sinning as a pattern of their daily life. They've called themselves Christians, but live as Sinners.

My heart breaks for our youth. Many times our youth are getting themselves wrapped up in bad habits, sinful behaviors and deadly addictions all because they don't know Jesus, but are searching for Him so deeply.

Ellen White G. White writes this:

"In order that the work may go forward in all its branches, God calls for youthful vigor, zeal and courage. He has chosen the youth to aid in the advancement of His cause. To plan with clear mind and execute with courageous hand demands fresh uncrippled energies. Young men and women are invited to give God the strength of their youth, that through the exercise of their powers, through keen thought and vigorous action, they may bring glory to Him and salvation to their fellow men" (*Evangelism*, p. 478).

Ellen White also went on to say that:

"There is nothing that Satan fears so much as that the people of God shall clear the way by removing every hindrance, so that the Lord can pour out His Spirit upon a languishing church and an impenitent congregation. When the way is prepared for the Spirit of God, the blessing will come" (*Review & Herald*, March 22, 1887).

Before people can want to clear the way for God's Holy Spirit to fill them, they've got to truly want to know, love and trust Him as their Savior and Lord.

The writer of Hebrews wrote:

> . . . So we must get rid of everything that slows us down, especially the sin that just won't let go. And we must be determined to run the race that is ahead of us. We must keep our eyes on Jesus, who leads us and makes our faith complete.

He endured the shame of being nailed to a cross, because he knew that later on he would be glad he did. Now he is seated at the right side of God's throne! So keep your mind on Jesus, who put up with many insults from sinners. Then you won't get discouraged and give up (Hebrews 12:1-3, CEV).

If and when our youth catch the vision that God has for them, their lives and their world, then what E.G. White said will begin to happen: "With such an army of workers as our youth, rightly trained, might furnish, how soon the message of a crucified, risen, and soon-coming Savior might be carried to the whole world! (*Education*, p. 271).

Chapter 3: What Teens Want & Need!

I believe that our kids can comprehend--and crave--deep, applicable, real-life biblical teaching from someone who not only knows the information, and can teach it effectively, but more importantly, someone who is striving to daily genuinely live it out as well! I believe that our youth spend too much time being entertained by both the world--and the church!

Let me be clear: I am CONVICTED that our youth need Jesus today more than any other time in this world's history! First, our youth need a real and vibrant saving relationship with Jesus today, additionally, they also need to know what they believe, why they believe it, how to live it and finally, how to explain and share it with others in such a way that they are distinctive, different, but not WEIRD!

But that's not all, our youth are Hungry! They are hungry for something to fill the collective holes in their souls that they are longing for. They are spending their time spinning their spiritual, relational and, emotional wheels looking all over this world for the joy and peace that only living a life with and in Jesus can give them and in the process they are getting themselves involved in sin, unhealthy and dysfunctional habits, relationships, lifestyles, disease and addictions.

Ultimately, they are unable to be the best that they can be for God and for themselves. So, instead of youth offering their bodies up to God as living sacrifices so they can test God's pleasing and perfect Will (Romans 12), they end up offering their bodies up to sin, unhealthy/dysfunctional lifestyles patterns, bad habits, disease, addictions, the world, and ultimately the devil. What a waste! It breaks my heart!

Youth are not only HUNGRY, but they are also HURTING and need connection! They need to connect with parents, teachers, Youth Pastors, Pathfinder leaders & adults who are not only unconditionally loving towards them, but who are also striving to live a Godly joyous Christian life AND who will connect with them consistently and honestly with them about their life experiences, both past and present.

Youth have six burning questions that they need answered:

1. Security: Who can I trust?

2. Identity: Who am I?

3. Belonging: Who wants me?

4. Significance: Do I matter?

5. Purpose: Why am I here?

6. Competence: What do I do well?

As a counselor I believe in speaking and writing plainly to our teens and teaching them clear Biblical truth and principles, couched in today's cultural context that is free of fluff and mindless references to entertainment! I find that teens crave and even appreciate a straight shooter. They can smell a fake a mile away. It is not my goal to shock and if I entertain—that's a bonus! God has asked me to spread the gospel, advocate, inform, encourage, educate, equip, and even rebuke when appropriate, through the ministry of community counseling that He has given me. I don't believe in guilting or shaming teens, nor will I attempt to convict them…that's the Holy Spirit's job. I believe our teens are intelligent enough to listen to, discern, and apply to their lives what is being said and to make wise decisions when given the appropriate information and support.

Over the years, I have seen the results of what Dr. Chap Clark in his book, *Hurt: Inside the World of Today's Teenagers* rightly terms "systematic abandonment." The systematic and near-total purposeful or unintended multi-dimensional abandonment and support of our teens by every demographic and people group that they felt were important to their total healthy development.

This leaves many of them naturally angry, feeling abandoned and gun-shy towards wanting to have any kind of close relationship with anybody—much less someone who represents an authority or parent figure in their life…and we wonder why our teens don't have any interest or impetus for wanting to know about, much less build a relationship with God.

There is a crucial principle that needs to be understood in understanding why our youth have such a difficult time connecting with God. The Apostle John wrote about it in 1 John 4:20 " . . . We cannot see God. So how can we love God, if we don't love the people we can see?" (CEV) Our youth can't love and trust others, because they have never felt loved by others in their lives. You see, when we are loved well, we basically learn that we can love, are loveable, and we are secure, significant and safe; and by extension, the world and others are safe. But if we are not loved well…if we're thrown to the wolves, like this generation has been, to fend for themselves, then they quickly learn that the world and others aren't safe.

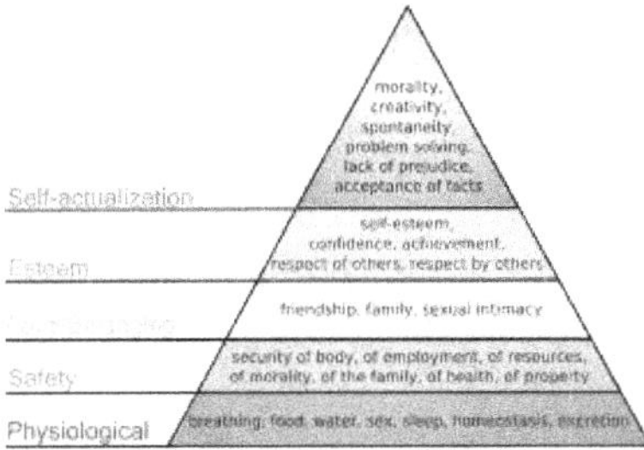

The diagram above is based on the American Psychologist, Abraham Maslow's "Hierarchy of Needs" model, it appears that the large majority of our teens can't reach the top layer of their life (Morality, creativity, problem solving, etc.) because they haven't been able to get the bottom four layers of their needs met effectively and consistently.

They've been used and abused and ignored and done wrong by so many people that they just don't think anybody cares about them…so in turn, they don't care about themselves, they don't care about anybody else, they don't care about stuff…they just don't care. They live in a world and culture that is image-rich, feelings-focused, and all about the here and now. They don't think about the future and usually have a difficult time making discerning, mature, wise, long-term decisions.

With this being said, as I've discussed above, the foundation must be laid of connecting teens with adults who are serious and sold-out to Jesus and who are consistent and honest about giving teens a rock-solid and vibrant connection and daily experience with Jesus.

Then that must be coupled with unconditional loving support and transparent mentoring and modeling of a joyful, Christian life from ALL or as many adults in their lives.

Lastly, there must be restorative, unconditional love couched within appropriate and correct teaching to strengthen, educate, and inspire our youth for an effective, joyful, Christian life of service to God, their Christian brothers and sisters and finally, the world!

I want to share below my perspective on teen spirituality. I find it closely mirrors their physical relationships as well. What I've seen in my experience is that when a teens' perspective on and about God is correct, their other relationships will follow suit. To that end, here are my observations:

Miranda Model of Formation of Adolescent Spirituality (2013)

Relational	Spiritual	Corresponding Feeling/Emotion
Stranger	Hear/Know About God	Hatred/Skepticism
Acquaintance	Meet/Introduced to Jesus	Confliction/Ambivalence
Familiar	Get Acquainted with Jesus	Caution/Wariness
Friendship	Beginning Friendship	Hope/Excitement
Close Friendship	Belief	Trust/Respect
Heart Friendship	False Obedience: follow rules b/c have to	Sacrificial Love
Marriage	Acceptance of Salvation/Baptism: follow rules b/c should	Interdependence
True One-ness	Conviction/True Obedience: follow rules b/c want to	Symbiosis

Chapter 4: Fixing What's Broken (From a Christian Perspective)

I say that this information is soley from a Christian perspective, but in my experience, many—if not all—of these solutions are common sense and teens of all religious persuasions have positively responded to them.

Dr. Roger Dudley, in his wonderfully insightful book, *The Complex Religion of Teens* writes:

"What are some things that adolescents need that we adults may have difficulty understanding?

1. Time to think and daydream—to develop abstract thinking—to question values.
2. Time to scream—we need to love them through the period of turmoil, no matter how trying.
3. Time for privacy—time away from parents.
4. Time to explore their sexuality.
5. Time to form a philosophy of life.
6. Time to consider the claims of Jesus Christ on their lives.

What are some of the things we need as adults as we try to understand and help adolescents?

1. To recognize in ourselves the tendency to be intolerant and threatened by evidences of independence in youth.
2. To understand the effect of rigidity and overcontrol on the need for adolescent independence.
3. To recognize the crucial difference between morals and mores (customs).
4. To understand the key role that modeling plays in making religion attractive to youth" (pp. 126, 127).

Dr. Roger Dudley posed this question to youth in his book *Why Our Teenagers Leave the Church*: " . . . If you could design the ideal Adventist congregation, what would it be like? Out of the hundreds of answers several themes emerged" (p. 194):

*   friendly and caring
*   deep spirituality
*   like a family
*   involved in community and mission
*   a thinking climate
*   young people involved

- meaningful worship
- diversity

I find it laughable that I talk to lots of different people from the highest levels of leadership in many different Christian (and non-Christian) organizations all the way down to folks like parents and volunteers and they all tell me pretty much the same thing "Omar, who can know what young people need these days…it's so discouraging!" Well, Christian teens pretty much just put their hearts on a platter for us and told us what's most important to them in a church (and this is important for non-Christian teens, too!), now the only question we have to answer is "Will we respond?" It seems to me that if we as a church endeavor to do these things, from our heart, that we will be able to decrease the terrifyingly high number of teens that are leaving our church these days (and will add to the number of the church).

Dave Kinnaman, author of the eye-opening book, *You Lost Me*, writes that what we as a church need to do to keep our youth and bring back the ones that have left is to give them courage. Specifically he wrote that the church needs to give our youth the courage to:

- Be pure: like Daniel and his three friends, they pre-decided to live for God—no matter what--in a difficult, complex, and depraved culture
- Be proximate: the courage to stand up for self-righteousness within the church. To find a way that connects Jesus to and in the world that we live in.

Kinnaman went on to state that it's the church's job to reverse the fifty-nine percent by consistently doing four things:

- The church must have a realistic and a right view of today's culture, what he called *cultural discernment.* He cited the Biblical verse in 1 Chronicles 12:32a " . . . from Issachar, men who understood the times and knew what Israel should do . . . (NIV)
- Building meaningful relationships with youth/young adults
- Begin *reverse mentoring* and *life modeling*: that is to allow a youth/young adult to lead them and orient them into their world. Also, he felt that young Christians turn into the Christians that we as Christians presently are…they become who we are in the very best and worst of it.
- Vocational discipleship: young people are so hungry to understand what they are called to do in life because they want so badly to make a difference for and to the world.

Lastly, Dr. Kara Powell & Dr. Chap Clark from Fuller Theological Seminary's "Sticky Faith" Movement state in their book, *Sticky Faith*, that it takes teenagers a minimum of 5 close healthy emotional connections with adults in order to not only get them through early adulthood/college but also to solidify their faith and likely make it stick for life.

Dr. Chap Clark, in his book, *Hurt 2.0: Inside the World of today's Teenagers,* provides a framework for reaching teens for Jesus.

One of the main reasons for the retreat of adolescents from the adult world beneath is that many adults have let them down throughout their lives. If adults are willing to wade through this lack of trust, and if they honestly desire to come alongside and nurture adolescents as they make their way into the community of adults, it will not take long for adolescents to recognize their sincerity and allow these adults into their lives.

The only qualification an adult needs is the willingness and fortitude to authentically care. Once this foundation is laid, adults can focus on the three specific needs of mid adolescents:

1. Youth need refocused, nurturing organizations and programs.

2. Youth need a stable and secure loving presence.

3. Youth need to experience authentic, intimate relationships with adults.

He also talks about five strategies to turn the tide systematic abandonment:

1. Those who work with youth should be trained in the changing youth culture.

2. Those who serve adolescents must work together.

3. Those who serve adolescents must understand youth and provide boundaries.

4. Parents need to be equipped and encouraged to parent the changing adolescent.

5. Communities must make sure that each student has a few (at a minimum: 5) adult advocates/mentors who know and care for him/her and should train and encourage others how to connect with them.

Chapter 5: The Elephant in the Room

For years I've been using the Bible as my ultimate rulebook and guide for truth within the scope of my counseling practice. And I can truly say that in over 20 years of counseling—with all ages—but specifically kids and teens, I've never, NEVER received a complaint/angry response related to it's inclusion in therapy. Why? It's simple really: clients who willingly come to see me (and that's a few and far between) and/or who are compelled—the legal word is "mandated" aka forced to see me are all ultimately searching for peace, purpose, joy, direction, and focus in their life. They may not yet know it, but they are all—we are all—searching for God!

I do not push my beliefs on my clients and I certainly don't proselytize. I am always respectful of each of my clients' beliefs and values and morals. When I do get around to introducing Bible truth, it's always after they proactively they proactively bring it up. When they do—and sooner or later they always do, I ALWAYS fully disclose that the information I am sharing comes out of the Bible, but I present/package it in a way that appeals to their inherent selfishness and strong need to live a pain-free life. My clients usually come to me after they've had years—if not a lifetime—of trying coping skills that are unhealthy and don't bring them the peace and results that they are looking for. I present the truths and principles of the Bible as simply "another coping skill" that they should try.

If they don't like it or don't think it works, then they are welcome to work with me to explore alternate coping skills. I don't try to make them a Christian, although I believe that if they were a Christian, their lives would be better off, but just adhering to the truths, principles and wisdom of the Bible will make their lives happier and healthier.

Additionally, I don't purposely use Bible lingo like sharing the actual name of the author or the name of the book. I do, however, give the client the context for the book, passage, or section of the Bible that I am assigning to them. I don't even initially suggest that they get their own copy of the Bible. I typically print off whatever section it is I'm assigning and ask them to review it and journal on it and we talk about it the next session, etc. God promises that anytime His Word, the Bible is shared, it will never be wasted and will always be fruitful! (Isaiah 55:11)

I am a Christian—meaning I am a follower of Jesus Christ--and that is the truth and worldview that I subscribe to. I don't adhere to the teachings of the Bible simply because I believe that they are true, and work in real life. No, I subscribe and follow the teachings of the Bible because Jesus did…and He predicted His own death and resurrection…and then pulled it off! My money's on Him!

I believe in the power of Biblical truth—specifically Wisdom literature in the Old Testament (Psalms, Proverbs, Job, Song of Solomon & Ecclesiastes) and find that specific books/portions of the Bible are more useful than others, although reading the Bible is a practice that always brings rich rewards. What I love about most of the Old Testament is the relevant stories about real people with real problems trying to make decisions—and how things really turned out. Teens are very interested in stories and the more stories you can share with them, the better. For some reason they don't feel that you are "attacking" or "judging" them directly and stories offer them an opportunity for you to ask them what they would have done in those specific situations.

However, in my estimation, specifically, the best portions for counseling are as follows:

1. Jesus' Sermon on The Mount: Matthew 5-7

2. The books of: Genesis; Joshua; Judges; 1 & 2 Samuel; 1 & 2 Kings; 1 & 2 Chronicles; Romans: specifically chapters 1, 5-8 & 13; 1 & 2 Corinthians; 1 Thessalonians chapters 4 & 5; 2 Thessalonians; Philippians; Galatians; Colossians; Ephesians & James

Many times my clients will begin to feel more comfortable with their existential questions about God (typically they have a lot of conflicted feelings about God related to some sort of trauma(s) that they or their families suffered and are trying to make sense of them all) and will begin to verbalize their thoughts and feelings about religion and spirituality in general and in their own life.

I, being a Lay-Pastor am totally comfortable addressing their concerns and feel that the therapeutic setting is the perfect setting to deal with these issues, but I counsel you that if you are not a Pastor, or Lay-Pastor, it's likely best to briefly address it and then refer the client to their local pastor. However, it's highly likely that the client may not attend a church or have a pastor of their own. In that case you can offer to assist the client in doing research on local pastors and/or offer to, during the actual session, work closely with the client in order to research and discuss the client's spiritual questions. Several trustworthy websites are:

1. http://timeline.biblehistory.com/home

2. https://www.amazingfacts.org/about-us/bible-questions

3. https://www.amazingfacts.org/bible-study/free-online-bible-school

4. https://www.itiswritten.com/forms/201/form_submissions/new

5. https://www.voiceofprophecy.com/bible-studies

After all, if this is the key underlying issue that has been causing the client untold problems (sometimes for years), addressing it would be highly therapeutic to the client and in his/her best interest.

Chapter 6: Mental Health Benefits of Faith & Religion

I could tell you all sorts of incredible and miraculous stories about the positive power of religion and faith in my own mental health, and in my clients' mental health (in fact, that's why I wrote this book), but I think it's best that you hear it from the actual researchers:

> Numerous studies have pointed out the beneficial influence of religion on mental health. As a 2015 review of the literature on the topic illustrates:
> [I]n general, studies of subjects in different settings (such as medical, psychiatric, and the general population), from different ethnic backgrounds (such as Caucasian, African American, Hispanic, and Native American), in different age groups (young, middle-aged, and elderly), and in different locations (such as the United States and Canada, Europe, and countries in the East) find that religious involvement is related to better coping with stress and less depression, suicide, anxiety, and substance abuse.
> Similarly, research published in 2006 found that there is an overwhelming positive relationship between religiosity and numerous *measures of emotional well-being*. According to the study:
> Most studies have also found a positive association between religiosity and other factors associated with well-being such as optimism and hope (12 out of 14 studies), self-esteem (16 out of 29 studies, but only one with a negative association), sense of meaning and purpose in life (15 out of 16 studies), internal locus of control, social support (19 out of 20) and being married or having higher marital satisfaction (35 out of 38).
> What is more, congruent findings were determined by a 2015 review examining over 3000 scholarly articles for the *International Journal of Emergency Mental Health and Human Resilience*, which found a "positive effect" of religion/spirituality on a variety of health outcomes, including: "minor depression, faster recovery from depressive episodes, lower rates of suicide, less use, abuse and substance dependence, greater well-being, and self-reported happiness."[3]

Chapter 7: Useful…and Not so Useful Theories of Psychology & Counseling

"No way! Check this out!" I loudly exclaimed. Many years ago, while at the Adventist Book Center, I stumbled upon an Ellen White compilation I'd never even heard of: *Mind, Character, and Personality.*

My wife looked at me, hit my elbow, and shushed me. Apparently I was being too loud. I couldn't help myself; I was excited! In that instant I had found the thrilling combination of my favorite topic written on by my favorite author. I felt like I had won the Adventist lottery of being the first table called at potluck!

As we drove home, my wife read to me from my newfound treasures…and I finally learned how God, writing through Ellen White, *really* felt about psychology and counseling.

<u>Excited? Not So Much…</u>
I still remember the day when I told my parents I was interested in psychology as a career. The look on their faces and their amalgamated level of excitement reminded me of how I felt when, many years ago, on Christmas morning, I tore into my *first* present, only to find…a six-pack of tube socks!

I've come to realize that my parents' lack of…shall I say, "enthusiasm"…about my choice of careers reflected many Seventh-day Adventists' feelings about psychology in general and counseling specifically.

Now, I understand why folks' antennas go up whenever someone speaks of psychology as a whole, because, although I took several psychology courses at one of our fine Adventist universities, I was largely educated and trained by a secular university. Since then I've received training and several post-graduate certifications from various Christian organizations.

However, as I was going through my undergraduate program, I never once stopped to think critically about how God viewed psychology. It wasn't until I was in graduate school, studying counseling, that I truly began to investigate God's perspective on the multiple theories of psychology, personality development, and counseling that I was studying. Initially, I did it not so much because the question kept me up at night, but because I was attempting to allay the fears of prospective conservative Christian clients.

As I began to honestly and purposely hold up these ideas and principles—worldviews, really—to the perfect truth of God's revealed counsels in both the Bible and Ellen White's writings, I was amazed by what I learned.

I expected the Bible and Ellen White to basically stomp psychology and counseling, but I found the opposite to be true. Both sources elevated these disciplines of study, but clearly warned that they, like any other academic discipline, divorced from a core underpinning of who God is and His position in our lives, could be warped and used inappropriately.

So what *do* the Bible and Ellen White have to say about psychology and counseling? What, if any, schools of thought or larger theories of psychology and counseling merge well with a Seventh-day Adventist Christian worldview? And further, how can these psychological theories accent and assist our spiritual walk or hinder and harm it?

Ellen White and Psychology
In Ellen G. White's lifetime (1827-1915), psychology—the science that studies the mind, its powers and functions, and how it affects human behavior—was in its infancy (*Mind, Character, and Personality,* vol. 1, p. 2). However, that didn't stop her from making these surprisingly clear and positive statements about its primacy:

- "To deal with minds is the greatest work ever committed to men" (*ibid.*, p. 4).
- "To deal with minds is the nicest work in which men ever engaged" (*ibid.*, p. 3). (In this context, "nice" means "delicate; requiring utmost care, accuracy, and skill.")
- "It is the duty of every person, for his own sake and for the sake of humanity, to inform himself in regard to the laws of life and conscientiously to obey them. All need to become acquainted with that most wonderful of all organisms, the human body. . . . They should study the influence of the mind upon the body and of the body upon the mind, and the laws by which they are governed" (*ibid.*, p. 3).

I've been involved in psychology since 1990 and counseling since 1996, and I agree with her: a basic understanding of psychology and counseling is crucially important for all Christians—even if we *never* speak to a counselor, therapist, psychologist, or psychiatrist. "But why?" you may ask. Simply put, it helps us all to be more effective soul-winners. When we understand the basics of what makes people tick, we can be wiser and more discerning in how we "bait our hooks" as we fish for men for the Master.

Not All Ponies and Rainbows
Before you go thinking that Ellen White has nothing but praise toward psychology, she feels just as strongly about its dangers:
> In many cases the imagination is captivated by scientific research, and men are flattered through the consciousness of their own powers. The sciences which treat of the human mind are very much exalted. They are good in their place, but they are seized upon by Satan as his powerful agents to deceive and destroy souls. His arts are accepted as from heaven, and he thus receives the worship which suits him well. . . . Through these sciences, virtue is destroyed and the foundations of spiritualism are laid. (*ibid.*, p. 20)

Specifically, she says, "It is the special work of Satan in these last days to take possession of the minds of the youth, to corrupt their thoughts, and inflame their passions" (*ibid.*, p. 22).

As Ellen White implies, many—even the majority of—psychological and counseling theories *are erroneous*! You may think this is a harsh statement, but after studying and being involved in both fields for more than twenty-five years, I've learned that we need to be discerning and careful about what we allow into our minds. These wrong and dangerous theories are largely based upon two erroneous worldviews:

1. The idea that human beings are basically good. This is called "humanistic psychology" or "secular humanism." Many people in this camp believe that:
- humanity as a whole is inherently good;
- we have within us all we need to be the best that we can be;
- as time progresses, we evolve and become even better.

They subscribe to the principle: "What the mind can conceive, the mind can achieve."

2. The closely related idea that there is secret untapped potential in each of us, and with specific training/mentorship, each of us can rise to our full potential. This idea is rooted in eastern religions and is a hallmark of such practices as hypnosis (what Ellen White termed "mesmerism") and many theories of psychology, personality, and counseling. Specifically, person-centered counseling, positive psychology, and Jungian psychology are centered in occult practices and thinking. We'll look at each of these practices and theories in turn.

Part 1: The Bad Side
Hypnosis
Author Dan Delzell writes, "Altered states of consciousness and other mystical practices open doors in the spiritual realm. Once a door is opened, a person becomes vulnerable to any spirits which come through that door." He recognizes the crucial fact that Franz Anton Mesmer, the founder of hypnotic therapy (hence the term "mesmerism"), was a practitioner of the occult.

Delzell continues:
> Hypnosis is basic to the Eastern religions. Prominent hypnotists have estimated that there are probably over 100 different stages of hypnotic trance. Christians should never allow themselves to be put in a trance….regardless of who is leading you into that mental state of relaxation. No matter what obstacles we face, God will help us if we rely upon Him rather than magical or mystical experiences. It is very dangerous to open hidden spiritual doors through hypnosis.[4]

Practically speaking, anytime you place yourself into an altered state of consciousness, you are giving up control and letting down boundaries—boundaries that God has put there for your own protection.

Person-centered/Client-centered Counseling
This is a key counseling approach under humanistic psychology. The founder, Carl

Rogers, believed that the best person to understand the client (the person receiving the counseling) is the actual client. He summarized his theory like this:

> It is that the individual has within himself or herself vast resources for self-understanding, for altering his or her self-concept, attitudes and self-directed behavior—and that these resources can be tapped if only a definable climate of facilitative psychological attitudes can be provided.[5]

Rogers felt that it was important to give the client what he called "unconditional positive regard" in an effort to make the counseling environment so nonthreatening and comfortable that the client would come to their own conclusions about what they believed, felt, and should do. In other words, Rogers believed that the counselor shouldn't disagree with the client at all or come to any external judgments or conclusions that weren't those of the client—the counselor should simply listen to the client.

This type of counseling is dangerous because it is basically the postmodern cultural worldview wrapped up in a counseling theory. The theory is founded upon the idea that the client's feelings, thoughts, values, and emotions can never be challenged and are therefore—by default—"right."

The prophet Jeremiah laments, "The heart is deceitful above all things and beyond cure. Who can understand it?" (Jer. 17:9, NIV). The practitioner of this dangerous theory can only sit helplessly by and watch clients wallow around in their thoughts, feelings, beliefs, and values…only to hope that one day they come to the Holy-Spirit-inspired right conclusions.

Positive Psychology
Positive psychology is one of the newest branches of psychology to emerge. It focuses on how to help human beings prosper and lead healthy, happy lives. During the 1950s secular humanist thinkers such as Carl Rogers, Erich Fromm, and Abraham Maslow developed theories that focused on happiness and the positive aspects of human nature. While many other branches of psychology focus on dysfunction and abnormal behavior, positive psychology is centered on helping people find fulfillment, productivity, and purpose.

The basic problem with positive psychology is that, although the theory recognizes the importance of what these thinkers call "spirituality," it doesn't recognize the validity, exclusivity, joy, and power of a relationship with Jesus. Jesus Himself said, "I am the way, the truth and the life. No one comes to the Father except through me" (John 14:6, NIV).

The wisest man in the history of the world, King Solomon, in his diary, the Old Testament book of Ecclesiastes, writes in twelve agonizing but crystal-clear chapters of his own failed attempts at finding all the things that positive psychology advertises it can offer. He called his attempts "vanity!" The bumper stickers are true: "Know Jesus,

Know Peace; No Jesus, No Peace!"

Jungian Psychology
Carl Jung, one of the most influential psychologists of the twentieth century, was heavily involved in occult practices, and much of what he writes about can be most closely described as souped-up shamanism. His focus on the mystical and on dream interpretation is dangerous. Also, he admitted to placing himself—on a regular basis—in "trance-like" altered states of consciousness. Many of his theories are related to "insights" he had while he was in those states or gained through his careful immersion in and study into mysticism.

Although Jung rightly believed that we all have two basic forces of good and evil working and warring within us, anyone who is an observer of the human condition can clearly see this fact.
Now that we've looked at some unbiblical psychological theories, in Part 2 we'll search for psychological theories that *do* mesh with a biblical worldview.

Part 2: The Good Side
In Part 1 of this article, we looked at the importance of understanding the human mind as well as some ways Satan has twisted the study of the mind. Despite the many pitfalls in the field of psychology, as a Christian and counselor, I can use my discernment to recognize that there *are* some theories and principles of psychology and counseling that display hallmarks of biblical truth (praise God!). These can be paired with what the Bible says about effective life change to help the people I work with.

The question that any person who ministers to others—that's all of us—must answer is: "What is the theory of counseling that
    1. best matches what the Bible says in terms of life change and
    2. is most successful in creating positive and consistent life change in a person?"

Before that question can be answered, we must first answer this basic question: "How does a person change their behavior?"

The answer is this: if we change the way we think, we change the way we act. It's that simple! Well, it's simple, but not *easy*. It takes a lot of concerted effort and "reprogramming," so to speak, but it's possible and very effective.

Ellen White asserts:
> As a man "thinketh in his heart, so is he" (Proverbs 23:7). Many thoughts make up the unwritten history of a single day, and these thoughts have much to do with the formation of character. Our thoughts are to be strictly guarded, for one impure thought makes a deep impression on the soul. An evil thought leaves an evil impress on the mind. If the thoughts are pure and holy, the man is better for having cherished them. By them the spiritual pulse is quickened and the power for doing good is increased. And as one drop of rain prepares the way for another in moistening the earth, so one good thought prepares the way for

another." (*Mind, Character, and Personality*, vol. 2, p. 655)

The Power of Our Thoughts
An unknown—but wise person said--"Whether you think you can, or you think you can't—you're right."

After all my years in psychology and counseling, I have come to believe that the most important principle that encompasses both disciplines is that of the power of our thoughts; specifically, recognizing what they are and controlling and changing them. Entire schools of psychological thought, personality theory, and counseling practice are built upon this principle: that in order to change our behaviors, we must first change our thoughts. The counseling theory called Rational Emotive Behavior Therapy (REBT), or in more modern times Cognitive Behavioral Therapy (CBT), most closely matches this biblical idea.

Here's the basic concept behind CBT:
- Problems/events lead to
- Thoughts based on predetermined core beliefs, which lead to
- Feelings/emotions, which ultimately lead to
- Actions/behaviors.

When something goes wrong, we tend to already have a predetermined core belief about what that specific event represents to us. These core beliefs are formed within us by the family we're raised in or the experiences we've had in our lives. These beliefs may be negative and unrealistic, causing us to perceive the world from a standpoint of helplessness and powerlessness or a sense of being unworthy and unlovable. These disordered, distorted, and unhealthy beliefs cause similar thoughts. Those thoughts drive us to feel a certain way—typically not good—which then causes us to act or behave in a specific way—again, not good.

The biggest problem is that many of us *believe* we can't change anything, and thus we are doomed to a lifetime of unhealthy thoughts and negative experiences. When these beliefs lead to consistent negative thoughts, they will ultimately result in negative actions and entrenched behaviors, habits, and addictions—what Ellen White called "inherited and cultivated tendencies" (see *Messages to Young People*, p. 68, and elsewhere).

Demolishing Strongholds
The Bible also has a name for this specific type of belief/thought/behavior: a "stronghold."

> For though we live in the world, we do not wage war as the world does. The weapons we fight with are not the weapons of the world. On the contrary, they have divine power to demolish strongholds. We demolish arguments and every pretension that sets itself up against the knowledge of God, and we take captive every thought to make it obedient to Christ (2 Cor. 10:3-5, NIV).

Here, Paul clarifies the importance of thinking rightly and closely evaluating every thought that enters our mind. Why? Simply because Paul recognizes the primacy and power of our thoughts.

All of these principles are reflected in the theories of CBT with similar, self-explanatory terms such as "thought-stopping," "thought-evaluation," "thought-replacement," and "challenging negative thoughts." The Bible, Ellen White's writings, and CBT all champion the importance of training yourself to *think about your thinking* and learning to think rightly.

The truth is that we *can* change our thought patterns and our resulting behaviors, and here is where the Holy Spirit comes into play. To learn more about how to change your thoughts, you can check out a prior essay I wrote for a Christian magazine, called "Anxious . . . For Nothing?" (https://thecompassmagazine.com/blog/anxious-for-nothing). Ellen White also writes extensively about our thought life in *Mind, Character, and Personality,* volume 2, chapters 34 ("Thought Habits") and 35 ("Right Thinking").

Ellen White's "Laws of the Mind"
In her writings, Ellen White listed several governing principles or "laws" related to the mind. These laws are also affirmed by sound psychological/counseling theories.

1. By beholding we become changed (2 Cor. 3:18):
> It is a law of the mind that it gradually adapts itself to the subjects upon which it is trained to dwell. . . .It is a law both of the intellectual and the spiritual nature that by beholding [God's character as revealed in the Bible] we become changed. The mind gradually adapts itself to the subjects upon which it is allowed to dwell. It becomes assimilated to that which it is accustomed to love and reverence. Man will never rise higher than his standard of purity or goodness or truth. If self is his loftiest ideal, he will never attain to anything more exalted. Rather, he will constantly sink lower and lower. The grace of God alone has power to exalt man. Left to himself, his course must inevitably be downward." (*Mind, Character, and Personality*, vol. 2, p. 418)

2. The things we speak become realities. In counseling-ese, this is called a "self-fulfilling prophecy":
It is a law of nature that our thoughts and feelings are encouraged and strengthened as we give them utterance. While words express thoughts, it is also true that thoughts follow words." (*ibid.*, p. 663)

3. Some addictions cannot be tapered; they must be stopped with clear and direct force. In addictionology (the study of addictions), the term "cold turkey" is used. Jesus alluded to this principle when He said, "If your hand causes you to stumble, cut it off. It is better for you to enter life maimed than with two hands to go into hell, where the fire never goes out" (Mark 9:43, NIV).

Great harm is done by a lack of firmness and decision. I have known parents to say, You cannot have this or that, and then relent, thinking that they may be too strict, and give the child the very thing they at first refused. A lifelong injury is thus inflicted. It is an important law of the mind—one which should not be overlooked—that when a desired object is so firmly denied as to remove all hope, the mind will soon cease to long for it and will be occupied in other pursuits. But as long as there is any hope of gaining the desired object, an effort will be made to obtain it. (*ibid.*, p. 419)

A Christian Approach to Psychology
God, in His Word, warns us that we need to be "alert and of sober mind" (1 Peter 5:8, NIV). We need to learn the importance of thinking rightly and clearly about ideas and philosophies: "See to it that no one takes you captive through hollow and deceptive philosophy, which depends on human tradition and the elemental spiritual forces of this world rather than on Christ" (Col. 2:8, NIV).

Ellen White goes a step further and asserts that the Christian can effectively understand the workings of nature, including the human mind, only through the lens of God's Word:
- "The true principles of psychology are found in the Holy Scriptures" (*Mind, Character, and Personality*, vol. 1, p. 10).
- "The Christian alone can make the right use of knowledge. Science, in order to be fully appreciated, must be viewed from a religious standpoint" (*ibid.*, p. 16).

So we see that Ellen White perceived psychology not as contradictory but as *complementary* to the Scriptures. However, psychological practices such as hypnotism, transcendental meditation, dream interpretation, and other practices based in the occult/new age/eastern religions are not only ultimately ineffective but extremely dangerous as well.
If we aren't firmly grounded in Christ, we will be washed away by Satan's misuse of sciences pertaining to the mind. Ellen White warns:

> In these days when skepticism and infidelity so often appear in a scientific garb, we need to be guarded on every hand. Through this means our great adversary is deceiving thousands and leading them captive according to his will. The advantage he takes of the sciences, sciences which pertain to the human mind, is tremendous. Here, serpent-like, he imperceptibly creeps in to corrupt the work of God.

> This entering in of Satan through the sciences is well devised. Through the channel of phrenology [the detailed study of the shape and size of the cranium as a supposed indication of character and mental abilities], psychology, and mesmerism [hypnosis], he comes more directly to the people of this generation and works with that power which is to characterize his efforts near the close of probation. The minds of thousands have thus been poisoned and led into

infidelity (*ibid.*, p. 19).

The only theory of counseling I have found that matches the patterns and principles outlined by both the Bible and Ellen White's writings is CBT, which is the study and science of thinking about our thinking and learning to discern, substitute, and control our thoughts—in essence, retraining ourselves to think rightly. Learning to control our thoughts, through the power of the Holy Spirit, holds the key to effective, positive life change and sanctification.

God, through the Apostle Paul, reminds us that He wants us to use all available means to reach and minister to the lost in His name (1 Cor. 9). A basic understanding of both the dangers and the benefits of psychology and its various theories—specifically counseling theories—will enable us to reach out more effectively to a world in desperate need of the life-giving message of Jesus' love, grace, and salvation.

<u>Additional Resources</u>
Mind, Character, and Personality, vol. 1 (entire book available online for free)

Mind, Character, and Personality, vol. 2 (entire book available online for free)

Steps to Christ by Ellen G. White

Persuasion: How to Help People Decide for Jesus by Mark Finley. Ministerial Association, General Conference of Seventh-day Adventists (1994).

Kay Kuzma books: http://www.adventistbookcenter.com/authors/kay-kuzma andhttp://www.familymattersministry.com

James Dobson books: http://www.paperbackswap.com/Dr-James-Dobson/author/

Henry Cloud and John Townsend books: http://www.boundariesbooks.com

Jan Silvious books: http://www.jansilvious.com/shopping (two especially great ones are *Foolproofing Your Life* and *Look at It This Way*)

Chapter 8: My Personal Favorite Therapeutic Approach
My favorite therapeutic counseling approach is CBT but I find that a lot of the teens (and adults) that I've worked with don't have the necessary physiological brain development in order to be very thoughtful, think abstractly about themselves, their actions, others, and the world. This is due mainly to the traumatic experiences that have emotionally retarded their growth.

So I find that the seven most effective therapeutic approaches (in no specific order) are:
- motivational interviewing
- solution-oriented brief therapy
- reality therapy (kissing-cousin of CBT)
- play therapy—yes, even with my older teen clients, and psycho-education (I'll discuss that term in more detail, next)
- art therapy
- music therapy
- bibliotherapy

I've found that if I begin with these less higher-order cognitive-demanding approaches, little by little as the client's brains are healed, they are able to more effectively think abstractly and I can slowly but surely transition them into more CBT techniques.

The Psycho-educational Process
Counseling teens is initially heavy on psycho education. This process works well in the therapeutic process. I assign books/workbooks (no more than one chapter a week), worksheets, etc. These are a good way to give the client power and make them feel successful that they have learned information that we can then, in the course of the session, address how they have effectively incorporate the information into their lives.

Realistically, I don't get upset if they've "forgotten" to do their work in the first week. I find that teens are very scared and anxious about learning new information—even if it's something that may help them. That's just human nature. If that happens, address it gently but honestly with the client and offer to review the information in the session. Many clients will initially need their emotional "hands" held during this difficult transition time. That's okay. We are here to serve not only as their example, but also as their guide. I find that a three-ring binder with all the resources that I present to the clients, broken down into the three different sections (I'll discuss in the next section) is the most effective way to go. But some clients get overwhelmed with this amount of information so you can just keep it to a small three-ring binder and just add the information as you progress through the material.

Don't get frustrated or discouraged that it takes teens much longer on their time line or that they lack motivation to begin or stay focused on this process. They will inevitably be shocked at how much work it takes to change their habits and begin thinking rightly due to the fact that the culture makes them think and believe that they are no consequences for their behaviors and that they can do whatever they want to do.

Continue reminding them that choices have consequences and that if they want to live a healthy and happy life and be a citizen of the world they need to learn to treat others the way they would want to be treated. Remind them of the benefits they will personally receive when they choose to live by God's precepts—even if they don't become Christians! Many times you will have to keep appealing to their inherent self centeredness and selfishness in order to help them to stay focused… at least in the beginning of the process, until they can see an actual payoff for their hard work in therapy.

Chapter 9: Getting Down to Business

So in order to fix the problem I initially brought up, I suggest a specific three-pronged approach:

I. Teach them how to effectively and consistently connect with God

II. Teach them how to effectively and consistently connect with themselves

III. Teach them how to effectively and consistently connect with others

****

Assessment

You can't move forward in dealing with the real problem until you know what the real problem is. Of course, by the time a teen receives formal intervention(s) (i.e., alternative educational setting; therapy; psychiatric/psychological evaluation; community resources, etc.) they will likely already be exhibiting a multitude of external manifestations aka "acting out behaviors" of their internal needs not being met; these things can easily be witnessed by total strangers (remember the list I mentioned at the beginning in the introduction?). No, the actual assessment begins with a more detailed and specific "pre-test" assessment and I know of none better than the Search Institute's "40 Developmental Assets." It's got a TON of strong research that shows that they are effective! The assets are described as:

> . . . 40 positive supports and strengths that young people need to succeed. Half of the assets focus on the relationships and opportunities they need in their families, schools, and communities (external assets). The remaining assets focus on the social-emotional strengths, values, and commitments that are nurtured within young people (internal assets).[6]

I use this FREE resource by printing it out a minimum of three age-appropriate asset sheets (http://page.search-institute.org/40-developmental-assets); one for the teen (identified client), one for the parent/legal guardian; and one for the teacher who knows the teen the best. If you want you can print off more and give one to each stakeholder working with the teen but I have found that having too much information from folks who only have peripheral knowledge of the teen makes things more problematic.

Then I have everybody circle the ones that the group feels the teen already has. The ones that are un-circled are the assets that will need to be worked on/addressed in the treatment planning. It's that simple. I date the sheets and make a copy for each person who completes one and at the end of my time working with the teen/family I administer this same assessment again as a post-test. In theory, once the needed assets have been addressed, the second assessment should reflect the asset gaps.

1. 40 Developmental Assets (Pre-test): https://www.search-institute.org/our-research/development-assets/developmental-assets-framework/

Part I-Aimless

It's been my experience that teens in this generation have been indoctrinated with several what I like to call "meta-cultural lies." There are five of them:

1. They were not created, but rather evolved. This presupposes that there is not a belief in God (atheism); and if there is a belief in God, then He is perceived—at a minimum—from an agnostic perspective ("who really can be sure that there's really a God?") or from an deistic perspective ("if there's a God, He's not really interested in humanity...or in me, for that matter!) This principle is the natural outgrowth of the theory of evolution and shows itself most effectively in teens believing that...

2. Truth is not discovered, but rather it is created. This principle is a natural outgrowth of the post-modern movement. The belief that there are no absolutes in life and that everything is relativistic. Therefore, this generation's belief is: "if it works, it's true;" rather than the correct maxim of generations past: "if it's true, it works."

3. Choices have no consequences. When there are consequences in teens' lives, for the most part, they are absolutely shocked and surprised that those consequences are as serious and long-standing as they are. This is there response because the popular culture, driven by the media (news, radio, movies, video games, tv, books/magazines) don't focus on them and certainly don't paint a realistic picture of...well, reality.

4. There are no restraints. If you want to do it, there is no judgment. Do what you want, when you want! The message that today's teens receive from the culture-at-large is that life is all about getting as much as you can, from whomever you can, and never...NEVER having to apologize. If it feels good, do it!

5. Your own feelings are *always* right—no matter what anybody says to you! No one has the right to diminish your "narrative" or experiences.

When you combine these four over-arching cultural lies, teens are set up to fail! And they typically see any kind of common-sense correction as "judgment" or bias or even hatred leveled directly at them.

<u>Big Idea</u>

Don't know how to connect with God

<u>Problem</u>

1. No purpose

2. No vision

3. No mission

4. No future plans

5. No hope

<u>Solution</u>

Need existential questions answered

It seems that there are at least six burning questions that teens want answered:

• Security: Who can I trust?

• Identity: Who am I?

• Belonging: Who wants me?

• Significance: Do I matter?

• Purpose: Why am I here?

• Competence: What do I do well?

Resources to Fix Problem

1. Prior "Introduction" "Youth Ministry Model" information I shared on connecting teens with God. Explaining and describing their own existential questions, search, and the solution is very eye-opening for them. A useful and non-threatening resource I would suggest would be the two books by…yours truly:

A. *Searching: It's Not What, It's Who*: https://amzn.to/2LHMyxJ

B. *Picking the King's Brain*: https://amzn.to/2IUAlbm

2. Alex & Brett Harris' book: *Do Hard Things* https://amzn.to/2LG1BIc

3. Sean Covey's book: *The 7 Habits for Teens* https://amzn.to/2IZ5pTp

4. Sean Covey's book: *The 6 Most Important Decisions You'll Ever Make* https://amzn.to/2L67xJs

Success = Teens on "purpose"

Part II-Angry

In today's culture teens don't know how to connect with themselves because they are overwhelmed with white noise. So much so that their emotional circuits are overloaded—all the time! Tell me the last time you actually saw a teenager without some sort of device in their hand, ear, or paying attention to it.

Today's teenager has been taught to have absolutely no personal time for stillness, reflection, introspection, or silence. This culture has taught our teens the lie that the more you do, experience, and post, the better you are! That you have to be busy all the time—and if you're not, then you're a loser! I can't tell you how many times I've heard parents tell me that their teenager always complains about being "bored." As a result, today's teenager has, for the most part, lost the skill of having a deep internal life.

They are not responders to life and circumstances, but rather *reactors*. They don't know how they feel about anything and can only verbalize feelings in the most general and vague terms/verbiage. Many of them, due to early childhood traumatic experiences have been emotionally stunted in their growth; biologically they are an adolescent, but emotionally they are likely much, much younger. Of course this also deeply affects their ability to be effective with abstract thought. This is a necessary and crucial skill for living an effective life (and for academics in general), but my focus is simply on their spiritual/emotional lives.

King Solomon wrote "For as he thinks in his heart, so *is* he" (Proverbs 23:7a, NKJV). So the question begs to be asked: "what happens to people when they stop thinking?" The answer is that they live for the here and now and can't think about anything but the present—with no concern or plan for the future…for anything! That's why it's so important to give them the gift of knowing how they really feel about something…and everything.

<u>Big Idea</u>

Don't know how to connect with themselves

<u>Problem</u>

1. No emotional needs met

2. Lack emotional intelligence.

3. Lack impulse control

4. No insight, no internal monologue and can't think abstractly

<u>Solution</u>

1. Trauma-informed Care

2. Erickson's Psychosocial Stages of Development

3. Silence/Reflection/Introspection/Journaling

4. Emotional Intelligence: Daniel Goleman & Howard Gardner

5. Dr. Kathy Koch's *8 Great Smarts*

http://www.8greatsmarts.com

 http://www.8greatsmarts.com/assessment/

http://www.8greatsmarts.com/freebies/

6. 16-PF https://psychcentral.com/quizzes/personality/start.php

7. Dr. James McDonald: Learning to Think Differently:
https://www.youtube.com/playlist?list=PLUAZcopbVbUBykFx_GNZAZctu_yZOXxM9

<u>Success</u>

Teen can successfully/effectively connect with themselves

Part III-Animalistic

Today's teens, for the most part, have a very difficult time being unselfish, feeling sorry for others, and/or even comprehending or being interested in someone else's experience. They are simply out for themselves. They have been neglected by many of the most crucial and important adults in their young lives (parents/legal guardians/teachers/pastors, etc.) that they have lost all trust/faith in them (remember Dr. Chap Clark's definition of "systematic abandonment"?).

Because of this, they are simply living their lives constantly on "survival" mode. They don't ever have an opportunity to let their emotional (and very often physical) guard down. Sooner, rather than later, this mode becomes a way of life and they don't see a need for thinking about others, being unselfish, or feeling caring about anybody else but themselves because in their experiences, every single time they've allowed themselves to become vulnerable, someone has either dropped the ball or taken advantage of them and hurt them.

Many years ago I watched a movie called "Lord of the Flies." It was based off the popular, yet frightening book by the same name. The author does an incredible job of illustrating the conflict between two competing impulses that exist within all human beings: the instinct to live by rules, act peacefully, follow moral commands, and value the good of the group against the instinct to gratify one's immediate desires, act violently to obtain supremacy over others, and enforce one's will. When we look at the general teen culture, which impulse do you think has won out?

<u>Big Idea</u>

Don't Know How to Connect with Others

<u>Problems</u>

1. Lack basic needs met (safety, food, shelter, care)

2. Lack life skills

3. Selfish

4. Lack empathy/remorse

5. Lack "soft" skills

6. Lack work skills/work ethic

Solution

1. Casey Life Skills Assessment http://lifeskills.casey.org Free Assessment and training curriculum tools

2. Maslow's Hierarchy of Needs

3. Growing Leaders: Habitudes https://growingleaders.com/habitudes/habitudes-for-middle-and-high-school/

4. *What Color is Your Parachute?* https://parachute4teens.com

https://parachute4teens.com/index.php/bonus.html

5. Consistent Service to Others: Of course, in my estimation, connecting teens to their local church is the best way to teach them to unselfishly and consistently serve others, but you can also check out these organizations and information as well: https://www.learningtogive.org/resources/youth-service-organizations

Success

Teen can successfully/effectively connect with and care about others and find and keep a job.

Assessment

Administer 40 Developmental Assets (Post-test)

<u>Conclusion</u>

As a mental health provider or someone who just loves and has a heart for working with teens, you must remember that God has placed you in the life of that specific client and no matter what happens, never, NEVER give up on them! You may be the only person in their life who is loving, dependable, consistent, and non-judgmental. The power of therapy is indeed formidable, but more formidable still is what God can do—not through your ability, but—through your *avail*-ability.

May God bless you as you use these ideas, information, and resources as you, Like Jesus, ministered to God's children in His name (Luke 4: 14-18).

---

[1] Accessed on May 30, 2018 from https://www.hhs.gov/ash/oah/adolescent-development/mental-health/mental-health-disorders/index.html
[2] Accessed on June 3, 2018 from https://www.counseling.org/docs/trauma_disaster/fact_sheet_7-terms-to-know.pdf?sfvrsn=af3e0017_2
[3] Accessed on June 16, 2018 from https://ifstudies.org/blog/the-positive-effects-of-religion-on-mental-illness
[4] Accessed on May 30, 2018 from https://www.christianpost.com/news/hypnosis-and-yoga-open-hidden-spiritual-doors-75641/
[5] Accessed on May 30, 2018 https://simplypsychology.org/client-centred-therapy.html
[6] Accessed on May 29, 2018 from https://www.search-institute.org/our-research/development-assets/developmental-assets-framework/